Norman P. Fischer & Katrine Hütterer

Imagine and Grow Rich

Norman P. Fischer
& Katrine Hütterer

IMAGINE AND GROW RICH

Create the Life of Your Dreams

Should this publication contain links to third-party websites, we do not accept any liability for their contents, as we do not adopt them as our own, but merely refer to their status at the time of initial publication.

This book is also available in paperback.

First published in German under the title "Stell dir vor und werde reich" in August 2021.
Translation of the German edition by Katrine Hütterer.

2021 Norman P. Fischer & Katrine Hütterer
c/o skriptspektor e. U.
Robert-Preußler-Strasse 13 / TOP 1
AT - 5020 Salzburg

Production and publishing: Independently published
ISBN: 9798481115269
Cover design: Katrine Hütterer
Cover design and image: Canva

www.katrinehuetterer.com
www.team-huetterer.com

This work, including all its parts, is protected by copyright. Any exploitation is prohibited without the consent of the authors.

"Setting goals is the first step in turning the invisible into the visible."

Tony Robbins

CONTENTS

Introduction 7

What is Wealth? 11

Know What You Want! 13

The Main Ingredient 17

Your Personal Environment 21

Autosuggestion vs. Suggestion 27

The Art of Doing It the Right Way 31

The Real Secret 39

The Slightly Different Way 47

The Law of Assumption 53

The Four Most Important Steps 59

The Only Cause 63

State Akin to Sleep 71

Visualisation (Scene Technique) 75

The Letter from Your Future 79

Your Gratitude Journal 85

The Best Investment of All 93

Coaching – Sense or Nonsense? 95

Afterword 99

Recommended Literature 103

About Norman P. Fischer 107

About Katrine Hütterer 109

Introduction

"If you don't plan your life, someone else will and you'll live someone else's dream."
Paul Bragg

Dear reader!

We are delighted that you have discovered our book and have chosen to read it. It is our second writing collaboration (the first one was our book "Manifestieren mit Tabellen",[1] currently only available in German) and even though we worked together on this once again, Norman will speak to you in first person in the main part of the book, as the content of this book is largely based on his experiences.

---

[1] Hütterer, Katrine/Fischer, Norman P.: Manifestieren mit Tabellen. Ein praktischer Leitfaden für wirtschaftlichen Erfolg, Independently published, ISBN: 979-8519555661.

We suspect that you are one of those people who still have dreams. Who believe deep inside, no: who know, that there must be a way to realise these dreams. Who simply refuse to give up, no matter what "the others" say or think, but who have not yet succeeded (otherwise you would hardly be reading this book).

Maybe you have already tried a few things to make your dreams come true. Maybe you have fallen flat on your face, but got up again because you just can't or won't give up?

Maybe you have already been looking for advice and help elsewhere? Have you read many books, from motivational guides to the "secret" and esoteric bestsellers or the wishing and visualisation guides?

Perhaps you have attended courses, taken training classes, acquired certificates and dissolved blockages.

You have written journals and ordered from the universe.

You have been ploughing away at these issues for years, but unfortunately your life is still not the way you want it to be. Even though you did it the way it was described in these books and courses. But let's be honest, some of the instructions were quite cumbersome. Or you didn't know exactly what the author meant when you read them.

Well, we hope we can shed some light about getting rich and creating the life of your dreams with this book by not only presenting the true secret of success and explaining how to apply it, but also by giving you a few tips on what you should avoid if you want to become rich, successful and above all happy.

We wish you every success in creating the life of your dreams!

Katrine Hütterer & Norman P. Fischer

PS: Please, dear reader, have mercy. Katy translated this book into English herself. Perhaps the phrasing is not always perfect, but the message is the point: Use the key to success we have rediscovered to create your perfect life – it's easy and it works!

What is Wealth?

When they hear the term "wealth", most people naturally think first of their bank balance.

And there is nothing wrong with that. After all, it is much more pleasant to live with a lot of money than with little or no money at all.

The amount of money you have in your account has a significant influence on your living conditions, your diet, your leisure activities, and your holidays. Money is therefore an important building block for your general well-being.

But let's not forget that health, emotional balance, and a loving personal environment are also important components of a fulfilled life.

Just as you can be rich financially, you should make sure that you are also rich in health, joy, fitness, and love.

How many people were and are financially rich and yet completely impoverished in health and/or emotion. I recall Ebenezer Scrooge – the bitter old man from Charles Dickens' Christmas story, which I am sure you know. Even though it is a fictional character, Scrooge is a good example.

So, if you want to live a happy, fulfilled life, you'd better take care of all these areas.

Know What You Want!

"If you don't know where you are going, you might wind up someplace else."
Yogi Berra

So, what do you want to manifest? Maybe you will answer: my dream house, a million dollars or euros, not to be sick anymore, to get your ex back, a horse, a fancy car or something else.

But is it really about this one "thing"? Or is it rather that you believe, that if this desire were fulfilled, you would feel better? You would be happy?

But then, once it's fulfilled, shortly afterwards you have another (material) craving without really getting better.

The subtitle of this book is: "Create the Life of Your Dreams" - I really hope that your dream life consists of more than a few material objects or being with a "certain" person.

You should therefore seriously and calmly consider what you want to experience and live in the different areas of life. Take your time for it. The rest of your life is at stake. One day more or less will hardly matter.

Perhaps you would like to take notes and answer the following questions:

- How do you imagine a perfect relationship/marriage?
- How do you imagine your financial situation? (Assets, income, how do you earn your money, etc.)
- How do you imagine your ideal friendship?
- Where would you like to travel?
- How would you like to live?
- What hobbies do you want to pursue?
- Which sports would you like to practise?

- How do you imagine your health and fitness?
- How do you want to be perceived by others?
- How do you want to spend your free time?
- Who do you want to get to know?

... and so on – I'm sure you can think of many more areas to reflect once you get started.

In order to become rich, successful and happy, it is simply indispensable to first be very clear about *what you really want* for yourself and your life. Take your time for these reflections.

The Main Ingredient

"A quitter never wins – and a winner never quits."
Napoleon Hill

I often hear people say: "I tried this or that method, but it didn't work."

Remember: There is nothing to "try" about a universal law. It is a law of nature - like gravity. You don't try out whether gravity works. The point is to learn how to deal with it.

When you first saw the light of day, you started crawling after a while and then learned to walk.

Did it work right away? – Hardly.

Did you give up? – No, of course not.
And? Can you walk now? – Probably yes ...

But it took time. A few years later you went to school. Then it took some years until you could read and write so well that you were ready for the next school level.

If you learn a craft, it usually takes three years to pass the journeyman's examination. Then you need a few years of work experience and then again, a few more years of schooling until the master craftsman's examination.

Boris Becker started playing tennis at the age of five and was seventeen years old when he won Wimbledon for the first time. Michael Schumacher started karting at the age of four and became world champion for the first time at the age of twenty-four.

Almost every professional athlete started at a young age and trains every day. The same is true for artists.

Impressive in this aspect is the biography of the Austrian Arnold Schwarzenegger,[2] who first became a bodybuilder, then a Hollywood actor, and finally a politician in the United States of America.

Please note: all people who become successful in any way, spend years focusing on and sticking to their goal.

Then how can someone who wants to change his life expect to achieve this goal in a few weeks with one simple method like manifesting? Correct: Not at all!

The main ingredient to achieve lasting success is CONSISTENCY!

So, if you are not willing to invest at least four years, you might as well not do it. This will save you

---

[2] Schwarzenegger, Arnold: Total Recall: My Unbelievably True Life Story, Simon & Schuster, ISBN: 978-1451662443.

from telling the world after five months that the method to become rich and successful, which I will present to you in this book, does not work.

Your Personal Environment

"You are the average of the five people you spend the most time with."
Jim Rohn

Have you ever noticed, looking around the world, that people who spend a lot of time together are "similar" in some way?

Successful people are with successful people.
Beautiful people surround themselves with beautiful people.
Intellectuals talk to intellectuals.
Golfers meet golfers.
Sporty people are with sporty people.
Conservatives spend time with conservatives.
Leftists with leftists.
Fat people share their free time with fat people.
Couch potatoes hang out with like-minded people.

"So what?", you may think, "Birds of a feather flock together!"

This is not wrong, but only one side of the coin.

Panta Rhei = everything flows.[3]

In other words: everything is in motion. As long as those who are spending time together are moving in the same direction, everything is fine.

It can look different if someone from such a circle wants to change direction.

---

[3] The formula Panta Rhei (Ancient Greek πάντα ῥεῖ 'everything flows') is an aphorism traced back to the Greek philosopher Heraclitus, suggested by Plato (in the dialogue Kratylos), but first appearing literally in the late ancient Neoplatonist Simplikios, to characterise the Heraclitan doctrine, seen on Wikipedia, as of 21st of August 2021.

Imagine five overweight couch potatoes meeting at a friend's house at Christmas and watching Rocky videos[4] while eating chips and drinking coke.

After the protagonist, the boxer Rocky Balboa, becomes world champion for the first time, one of the five says: "Guys, we have to do something. No more hanging around, we're going to get in shape." The four others look at him and ask if he is not well, if everything is okay, or if he is on some illegal drugs.

But our motivated couch potato signs up at the gym on the second of January, trains from then on and changes his diet. Every Wednesday and Saturday evening, as well as Sunday afternoon, he meets his buddies to watch videos.

Of course, they offer him chips and coke and try to dissuade him from training. How long do you think

---

[4] This refers to the US film series about the boxer Rocky Balboa, see also https://www.imdb.com/list/ls031152077/, as of 21st of August 2021.

he will stick to his goal of getting fit if he stays in this circle of friends?

Fact is, that when someone tries to "leave" a group, the group usually does not want to let him go and tries to hold him back.

There are coffee parties where those who get together tell each other day in, day out about their aches and pains and thus produce further suffering.

You cannot become sober in a clique of drinkers; you cannot become a non-smoker in a group of smokers, or you will be at latent risk of relapse. You cannot become financially successful if all your friends are broke and have resigned themselves to it, and you cannot become an athlete if those around you are completely unsporting and eat the wrong food.

Why am I saying this so clearly?

Realise and deal with one thing: if you start to change your life, there is an extremely high probability that others will try to stop you. And if you continue your path, there is an extremely high probability that people around you will leave you or simply disappear.

That's not a bad thing, because in principle it runs through the whole circle of life: Your kindergarten friends might not get into the same primary school, primary school friends might not get into the same secondary school, people leave town to get an education or a job, people die. That is the course of life.

Know what you want, stay consistent and don't let others hold you back.

Of course, it is helpful to surround yourself with people who are on the same path or are already where you want to be. Certainly, there will be one or two people in your environment who think that what you are doing is nonsense. Therefore, it makes sense to look out for people who think like you do.

Autosuggestion vs. Suggestion

"Every day, in every way, I am getting better and better."
General purpose formula by Émile Coué

In his books about autosuggestion, the French pharmacist and psychotherapist Émile Coué reported how people have lost illnesses or changed their life circumstances through autosuggestion, i. e. through monotonous repetition of a certain formula - in Coué's case: "Every day, in every way, I am getting better and better".[5]

Autosuggestion has been intensively researched in recent years, and there are now numerous scientific experiments and, of course, self-experiments that

---

[5] For example: Coué, Émile: Self-Mastery Through Conscious Autosuggestion, G&D Media, ISBN: 978-1722502638.

make it clear that autosuggestion always has an immediate effect.

Many mental and motivational trainers also rely on autosuggestions such as "I can do it", "I'll achieve my goals ...!" and many more.

So, it is proven that our subconscious mind is programmable.

Let's assume that you sleep for eight hours and for another two hours you are so busy with yourself that nothing else can get to you. Now you can take an hour every day to programme your subconscious with your goals.

This means there are thirteen hours left for you to receive messages.

You turn on the TV, quickly enter a stupor and hear about wars, crises, disasters, diseases. Further you watch films including murder, theft, manslaughter, crime and more.

You drive around in your car or do chores (both of which are semi-automatic) and have the radio on. You listen to the news with a lot of bad news, advertisements for products that nobody needs and that don't help anybody, and "inspiring" music like "Highway to Hell", "He Hit Me" or "Pumped Up Kicks".

Even when you're standing at the cash register at the petrol station, the headlines on the newspapers jump out at you.

Remember: **You are programmable through your subconscious.**

If you don't programme it, others will. And these people are professionals.

Therefore, you should think carefully about what you feed your mind with or have it fed with.

Turn the TV off, leave the radio on mute, cancel the daily newspaper and the weekly journals.

Check out sources that you can select. If you want to listen to music, choose wisely what you listen to.

The Art of Doing It the Right Way

Until now you have learned something about the "framework". But what is *the method*, how did I, Norman, become successful? Let me share my story with you.

At times when things were not going the way I wanted, I started reading books. It all started with motivational literature. Everything should be possible, and you should break your limits, so they said.

Relatively quickly I realised that the cause of success or failure was buried deeper. The subconscious, which accounts for up to ninety-five percent of us, directs our lives.[6]

I was fascinated by the book "The Power of Your Subconscious Mind" by Doctor Joseph Murphy.[7] I experimented with the suggestions made in this work and had some initial success. However, the way Murphy recommended them was relatively cumbersome in my eyes and so the book ended up on the shelf after some time.

I also found "Think and Grow Rich" by Napoleon Hill very inspiring.[8] The author, who was given the task of finding out what the factors for success and

---

[6] You can find more about this topic here http://webhome.auburn.edu/~mitrege/ENGL2210/USNWR-mind.html or here https://sheroldbarr.com/harness-subconscious-mind-2/, as of 17th of September 2021.

[7] Murphy, Joseph: The Power of Your Subconscious Mind: Unlock the Secrets Within, TarcherPerigee, ISBN: 978-1585427680.

[8] Hill, Napoleon: Think and Grow Rich, Wilder Publications, ISBN: 978-1604591873.

failure are, had talked to hundreds of people and derived some things from them.

In his book he always speaks about a "secret" that is the cause of success. And there is no shortage of stories of successful people.

For example, there is the story of an old country doctor who sold a kettle, a wooden spoon, and a secret recipe to the pharmacist Asa Candler for five hundred dollars. The ingredients for Coca-Cola. The doctor sold the things because he did not see the right opportunity. Candler did.

Also the story of Henry Ford, who wanted an eight-cylinder engine from a block that his engineers told him was impossible. Ford remained determined, and in the end, he had his engine.

Although I have certainly read this book thirty times, the "secret" did not open to me, at least not in such a way that I could have understood it and put it into practice in my life.

What became clear to me, however, was that achieving goals and success had to work "somehow" differently than we are so commonly taught.

Salvation was at hand, supposedly with the book and the film „The Secret".[9] Well, the "secret" to happiness, success and wealth was finally going to be revealed. The author had spoken to various success coaches and people who had achieved extraordinary things, and they had each explained in their own words how they had achieved their goals.

How? – Yes, well, I didn't understand it exactly here either. You should imagine something, figuratively, and then feel how it feels. Hmmm, difficult. What does a house with a pool feel like? Wet?

---

[9] Byrne, Rhonda: The Secret, Simon & Schuster UK, ISBN: 978-1847370297.

In between, I read dozens of biographies of successful people. All of them inspiring, some of them very touching. Always from the point of view of the person who describes what he/she believes, why he or she was successful. Not in one book did I find a comprehensible, universally applicable method to create the life of my dreams, to achieve my goals and to be successful.

However, through the constant occupation with this kind of literature, something changed in my life. Sometimes I was successful with the things I set out to do, sometimes not. So, I guess I was unconsciously doing things right in some matters.

By the way, I am now convinced that most successful people don't even know exactly why they are successful. They simply do things in a certain way, as they were taught from an early age and don't know any different.

Later, in my search for the Philosopher's Stone, I remembered "The Secret". The author had talked about how she had been given a book by her daughter, that gave her hope when she was very unwell. This book had revealed „the secret" to her.

I don't remember how and where, but at some point, and somewhere I found the clue as to which book it was: A certain Wallace D. Wattles had already put it down on paper in 1915 in the USA under the title "The Science of Getting Rich".[10] In German (important for me) I found a version with the title "Das Gesetz des Reichwerdens". By the way, there is now also a newer translation for German speaking people of this great and inspiring book under the title "Die Kunst, reich zu werden" by my co-author Katrine Hütterer.

---

[10] Wattles, Wallace D.: The Science of Getting Rich, CreateSpace Independent Publishing Platform, ISBN: 978-1490471761.

Compared to new guidebooks, which come with hundreds of pages and subsequent volumes plus workbooks, Wattles' work seemed very manageable to me.

Basically, he explains that everything is created from the same substance and man can shape it into his or her desired form with the power of his or her thoughts. He cites imagination, faith, determination, and gratitude as the way to get there.

I noticed, even when reading other, older books about reaching your goals and being successful in life, that they were all relatively concise and simply written.

Modern literature about success, happiness and wealth was often filled with so many curves, bows and circumlocutions that the actual message was buried. Perhaps the authors thought that something that simple could no longer be sold today?

What was still missing for me was the *"how"*! How could I achieve what I wished for my life?

Then I came across "The Master Key System"[11] by Charles F. Haanel in its first German translation. The work was first published in 1912 and described exactly how to proceed to become successful. However, the "Master Key System" was originally intended and designed as a twenty-four-week correspondence course. I'm sure it was an excellent manual – but for me it was too cumbersome and time-consuming, just like the good old Joseph Murphy. After initial efforts, the "Master Key" was also relatively quickly too complicated to handle for me, and I gave up.

But there had to be something to this "secret" for success and wealth!

---

[11] Haanel, Charles F.: The Master Key System, SoHo Books, ISBN: 978-1612930831.

The Real Secret

By now I thought I had read pretty much everything about how to get rich and successful and happy - until I discovered *him*.

Somewhere while rummaging I found a paperback booklet, translated into German by I-BUX, originally written by a certain Neville Goddard including „Es ist bereits so" and „Genauso hatte ich es mir ausgemalt – Vom Erfühlten zum Erfüllten".

Goddard??? I had not come across the good man at all before. Why? Neville Goddard was a Christian mystic who had become a multi-millionaire himself by applying what he taught. He gave hundreds of lectures for small fees and this income he donated to the church. He sold his books for little money to the listeners of his lectures. No wonder that he was not mainstream.

I also found it interesting that Neville Goddard and Doctor Joseph Murphy had the same mentor: A rabbi named Abdullah, who came from Ethiopia and lived in the USA.

Neville Goddard taught: "Imagine specifically what you want, go steadily into the feeling of fulfilled desire and allow it to be realised in your world by believing in it."

Imagination is the only reality!

WOW! So, it's not about feeling the vibration of a twelve-cylinder engine under your butt - but the question must be: *"How would you feel if you were driving the twelve-cylinder car you wanted?"* And then, when you listen deep inside yourself, a feeling comes up. You might feel great, it might feel very touching, it might be the feeling of gratitude. But it doesn't vibrate. That's what it's all about!

I felt like I had finally found what I was looking for. The "Law of Assumption" was my Holy Grail!

Neville says everything that can exist already exists, and by going into the state of fulfilled desire, you bring it into your world.

"Everything is possible for one who believes."[12]

And: Don't worry about the "how"! Don't worry about how you get what you want, just let it happen.

This fitted perfectly with my favourite quote from Henry Ford:

"Whether you think you can, or you think you can't – you're right."

---

[12] See also in the Bible, Mark 9:23: https://biblehub.com/mark/9-23.htm, as of 18th of September 2021.

The more I thought about it, the more I realised that I had actually manifested the past events in my life (the beautiful and the unpleasant ones) by myself. Not all consciously, of course, but at least unconsciously.

In fact, there were also some events in my life so far that seemed absurd at first, but eventually became major successes that I could hardly explain to myself. This clearly spoke for Neville's statement: "Don't worry about the 'how'!".

I read my books from Neville a second, third and fourth time and imagined that it would be great to read and hear more of the Law of Assumption and get more concrete suggestions.

A few weeks later, when we were talking about books, a casual acquaintance asked me if I had ever heard of a certain Neville Goddard.

After I had not heard from him for tens of years, he was already present again!

When I asked her incredulously, "Where did you discover *him*?", she told me about a guy from Berlin who had translated some of Goddard's work into German and gave webinars about the LOA. So, I got hold of Kevin Kunert's books and became even more intensively involved with the subject.

Then I heard again and again about the "Complete Reader".[13] A compilation of Goddard's writings. Unfortunately, it was only available in English. I thought it would be pretty cool if I could read this anthology in German.

---

[13] Goddard, Neville: The Complete Reader, Audio Enlightenment; Illustrated Edition, ISBN: 978-0991091409.

It wasn't long before Daniel Daddeh appeared on the scene who had translated the entire book into my mother tongue. Exactly as I had imagined it!

In the time that followed, I met some people on the internet with whom I have been exchanging ideas about manifesting for years now. I also learned more from my co-author Katy, who lives and teaches manifesting with the Law of Assumption together with her colleague Yvonne.

They provide a lot of free content on their website, podcasts and YouTube channel and offer webinars, meditations, and online courses for successful manifesting. In their books, they explain the Law and how to make use of it, in simple and understandable terms.[14]

---

[14] https://www.team-huetterer.com/, as of 18th of September 2021.

If you have no previous knowledge about the Law of Assumption, I recommend the book "Simply Manifesting: The Law of Assumption Easily Explained" by Katy and her colleague Yvonne Kalb.[15]

Manifesting works exactly as Neville explains it.

That is the REAL SECRET:

Imagination is the only reality, and everything is possible to him or her who believes.

---

[15] Hütterer, Katrine/Kalb, Yvonne: Simply Manifesting: The Law of Assumption Easily Explained, Independently published, ISBN: 979-8476407959.

The Slightly Different Way

Before I had discovered Neville Goddard, I usually did things like this: I would have an idea about something, brood over it for a while, and then my mind would take over, evaluate it as "this will work" or "this won't work" and then I started implementing it - or not. Sometimes it worked out fine and sometimes it didn't.

Neville says that every wish already carries in itself the energy to fulfil it. Like a seed, which also already carries all the information to become a full-grown plant. It now seems to me a relatively stupid idea to cut open the seed and pluck out the plant!

Imagine you live in Cologne and want to visit your cousin Max Müller in Munich by car. You have never been to Munich before. What do you do? You program your navigation system and let it guide you.

You drive along the motorways and arrive at some point on the outskirts of Munich.

When you see the road sign at the entrance to the city, your mind says: "Ah, Munich! I know it from the television series. I'll find my way. I don't need an annoying navigation system!" – and you switch off the GPS.

Do you think you'll get to Max Müller in time? Probably not.

But this way of thinking and behaving seems familiar to you? At some point, our actionism, our intellect, kicks in and destroys the seed that has just sprouted.

There is a delightful cartoon on YouTube by Dieter Nuhr in which a cartoon penguin turns very slowly to the camera and says loud and clear (in German):

„If you don't have a clue, just shut the f**k up!"[16]

That is exactly the advice you should give your mind when it interferes again.

These thoughts were running through my head as I grappled with Neville and financial freedom.

I guess it was really time to try something different. So, in the morning and in the evening, I imagined that my account had a certain balance and my tax advisor asked me how on earth I had managed to arrive there so quickly.

I can tell you, it felt pretty great. Every morning and every evening.

A short time later, this happened:

---

[16] https://www.youtube.com/watch?v=5KT2BJzAwbU, as of 6th of August 2021.

NOTHING.

But since I was determined to give this Law of Assumption-thing a real chance, I just kept going steadily.

A few weeks later, I suddenly had the inspiration to ask a client for a bonus because I had successfully completed an order. It was a considerable sum that I proposed to him. And after two days of thinking about it, he called me and said: "You have earned it. Please write me an appropriate invoice!" - Three days later, the money was in my bank account.

Since then, I have achieved several successes in different areas and met many people who live and work in the same way.

And how exactly does that work now? What do you have to do?

The following chapters from "The Law of Assumption" to "Visualisation" are an excerpt approved by the authors from the book "Simply Manifesting – The Law of Assumption Easily Explained" by Katrine Hütterer and Yvonne Kalb.

This will give you an insight into working with Neville Goddard's Law of Assumption to create the life of your dreams.

The Law of Assumption

"Imagination is the only reality."
Neville Goddard

This is probably the most famous and important quote by Neville Goddard. Our imagination is the only reality. What does this mean for us? This phrase explains us that we are the only cause of the phenomena of our lives, because with the help of our imagination we can influence and control our reality and our external world ourselves. This simple, but for many difficult to accept, statement is basically the whole secret of the Law of Assumption. Everything that shows up in our lives, we have previously created ourselves during our lives through our assumptions and our imagination. What shows up in our outside world now are mostly the assumptions from the past. This is difficult for many people to acknowledge at first. However, the beauty of this universal law, which always works whether we use it consciously or (like most people) unconsciously, is that, conversely, we have absolute power over the phenomena of our lives.

We can decide at any time to intervene consciously and only create in our lives what we want to have and experience there. You will now learn how to do this most easily.

Neville put it this way in his lecture "Imagination Fulfills Itself": *"Believe that it is real. Believe that it is true and that it will happen. Imagination will not disappoint you if you dare to accept something and persist in your acceptance, because imagination will fulfil itself in what becomes your life."*[17]

Our life on the outside always expresses only our inner self-talk. What we think about ourselves, about relationships, about money, about health, about other

---

[17] http://realneville.com/txt/imagination_fulfills_itself.htm, as of 20th of March 2020.

people, and the world in general - or perhaps fear, but in any case, believe, assume, is also shown to us in our outer world.

Imagination is belief and vice versa. Most of what we believe about ourselves, and others has been suggested to us over many, many years - mostly unconsciously. We all know that critical voice in our head that makes us feel bad about ourselves or the world. These can be, for example, old beliefs from childhood or limiting assumptions of our society such as "You'll never achieve anything" or "You can't have it all". Sentences like "The world is not a safe place", "Money is the root of all evil" and many more are deeply embedded in us, usually without us being aware of it.

Make a long story short: We imagine and manifest twenty-four hours a day and even while we sleep. Think about it: What thoughts do you fall asleep with? Are you worrying? Are you still having an argument with someone in your imagination? Are you thinking about problems at work? About the children's bad marks at school? What does your self-talk sound like during the day? Is it different from the one before you go to sleep?

With these thoughts and the associated feelings that they trigger in us, we unconsciously create our reality all the time. Unfortunately, it usually does not correspond to what we would like to have and experience in our lives. Therefore, it should be clear by now: We must actively intervene and use the Law of Assumption in our favour, otherwise it will use us. We must therefore consciously change our self-talk and our assumptions in such a way that our ideal, our desired life can be realised. We must educate, re-educate, our beliefs and our imagination.

How do we achieve this best? With conscious autosuggestion[18] or self-persuasion, because it can – consistently applied – erase the old, unconscious beliefs and overwrite them with the new, desired ones.

The previously mentioned Émile Coué,[19] who is considered the founder of modern conscious autosuggestion, had this to say: *"Conscious autosuggestion, done with confidence, faith and perseverance, realises itself automatically."*

---

[18] Autosuggestion is the process by which a person trains their unconscious to believe in something.
[19] Émile Coué was born in Troyes (France) in 1857. He was a pharmacist and author as well as the founder of modern conscious autosuggestion. Coué died in Nancy (France) in 1926.

The Four Most Important Steps

1. Know exactly what you want. Become aware of your desire, your ideal state.
2. Create a simple and short imaginative experience (scene or sentence) that would imply that your wish is true. Something that would naturally follow the wish fulfilled.
3. Go into the state akin to sleep – meditation, silence, stillness.
4. Repeat this imagination constantly until it completely dominates your mind, until it feels true and real.

After the seed has been sown through conscious autosuggestion, it is of course important not to dig it up again through our doubts. Experts recommend at least thirty, but ideally sixty to seventy minutes of conscious autosuggestion per day.

With the Law of Assumption, one thing is very important, but also very difficult for most people to handle: The "how", the "who" and the "when" are not in our power and we cannot influence them. That means, how and when exactly our wish will be fulfilled and who will contribute in what way – we must not concern ourselves with that, that would dig up the seed again.

It is normal that we sometimes begin to doubt. This happens to all of us when we consciously apply the Law of Assumption, especially when success does not come immediately. But if we remain consistent and apply the LOA as a philosophy of life, we will eventually be able to free ourselves from our doubts sooner or later.

No matter what our desire is and no matter how many people it will take to make it happen, they will all get in motion to make it happen and it will seem perfectly natural to you. Neville once said: *"Looking back, it happened so naturally that you say to yourself, 'Well, it would have happened anyway', and you quickly recover from that wonderful experience."*

The Only Cause

"You are the cause of all the phenomena of your life."
Neville Goddard

An important aspect of the Law of Assumption is that we are the only cause of all phenomena in our lives. Far too often we create a secondary cause: we blame other people or circumstances for our problems. "My marriage could be great, but my husband won't work on it", "I'd love to, but I'm not fit enough" or "My job would be great, but my boss is just unbearable" are just a few examples of how we like to look for the reasons of our problems on the outside instead of our inner assumptions.

In "At Your Command", Neville wrote the following: *"Put not your trust in men for men but reflect the being that you are and can only bring to you or do unto you that which you have first done unto yourself.*

'No man taketh away my life, I lay it down myself.' I have the power to lay it down and the power to take it up again. No matter what happens to man in this world it is never an accident. It occurs under the guidance of an exact and changeless Law. 'No man' (manifestation) 'comes unto me except the father within me draw him,' and 'I and my father are one.' Believe this truth and you will be free. Man has always blamed others for that which he is and will continue to do so until he finds himself as cause of all. 'I AM' comes not to destroy but to fulfill. 'I AM,' the awareness within you, destroys nothing but ever fill full the molds or conception one has of one's self. It is impossible for the poor man to find wealth in this world no matter how he is surrounded with it until he first claims himself to be wealthy. For signs follow, they do not precede. To constantly kick and complain against the limitations of poverty while remaining poor in consciousness is to play the fool's game. Changes cannot take place from that level of consciousness for life in

constantly outpicturing all levels. Follow the example of the prodigal son. Realize that you, yourself brought about this condition of waste and lack and make the decision within yourself to rise to a higher level where the fatted calf, the ring, and the robe await your claim.

There was no condemnation of the prodigal when he had the courage to claim this inheritance as his own. Others will condemn us only as long as we continue in that for which we condemn ourselves. So: 'Happy is the man that condemneth himself not in that which he alloweth.' For to life nothing is condemned. All is expressed.

Life does not care whether you call yourself rich or poor; strong or weak. It will eternally reward you with that which you claim as true of yourself. The measurements of right and wrong belong to man alone. To life there is nothing right or wrong. As Paul stated in his letters to the Romans: 'I know and am persuaded by the Lord Jesus that there is nothing unclean of itself, but to him that esteemeth anything to be unclean, to him it is unclean.' Stop asking yourself whether you are worthy or unworthy to receive that which you desire. You, as man, did not create the desire. Your desires are ever fashioned within you because of what you now claim yourself to be. When a man is hungry, (without thinking) he automatically desires food. When imprisoned, he automatically desires freedom and so forth. Your desires contain within themselves the plan of self-expression. So leave all judgments out of the picture and rise in consciousness to the level of your desire and make yourself one with it by claiming it to be so now. For: 'My grace is sufficient for thee. My strength is made perfect in weakness.'

Have faith in this unseen claim until the conviction is born within you that it is so. Your confidence in this claim will pay great rewards. Just a little while and he, the thing desired, will come. But without faith it is impossible to realize anything. Through faith the worlds were framed because 'faith is the substance of the thing hoped for – the evidence of the thing not yet seen.'

Don't be anxious or concerned as to results. They will follow just as surely as day follows night. Look upon your desires – all of them – as the spoken words of God, and every word or desire a promise. The reason most of us fail to realize our desires is because we are constantly conditioning them. Do not condition your desire. Just accept it as it comes to you. Give thanks for it to the point that you are grateful for having already received it – then go about your way in peace.

Such acceptance of your desire is like dropping seed – fertile seed – into prepared soil. For when you can drop the thing desired in consciousness, confident that it shall appear, you have done all that is expected to you. But to be worried or concerned about the HOW of your desire maturing is to hold these fertile seeds in a mental grasp, and, therefore, never to have dropped them in the soil of confidence.

The reason men condition their desires is because they constantly judge after the appearance of being and see the things as real – forgetting that the only reality is the consciousness back of them. To see things as real is to deny that all things are possible to God. The man who is imprisoned and sees his four walls as real is automatically denying the urge or promise of God within him of freedom. A question often asked when this statement is made is; If one's desire is a gift of God, how can you say that if one desires to kill a man that such a desire is good and therefore God sent? In answer to this let me say that no man desires to kill another. What he does desire is to be freed from such a one. But because he does not believe that the desire to be free from such a one contains within itself the powers of freedom, he conditions that desire and sees the only way to express such freedom is to destroy the man – forgetting that the life wrapped within the desire has ways that he, as man, knows not of. Its ways are past finding out. Thus man distorts the gifts of God through his lack of faith.

Problems are the mountains spoken of that can be removed if one has but the faith of a grain of a mustard seed. Men approach their problem as did the old lady who, on attending service and hearing the priest say, 'If you had but the faith of a grain of a mustard seed you would say unto yonder mountain 'be thou removed' and it shall be removed, and nothing is impossible to you.'"[20]

By the way, Katy's colleague Yvonne describes this topic very impressively in her extremely honest book „Hoppla, ich bin die einzige Ursache… für die Phänomene meines Lebens" (currently only available in German).[21] She writes about how much she got bogged down by her negative assumptions, how much she repeatedly made others, the circumstances of her life, fate, the cause of her problems, her fears, and compulsions.

---

[20] http://nevillegoddardpdf.com/free-books-and-lectures/neville-goddard-free-pdf-at-your-command/, as of 13th of September 2021.
[21] Kalb, Yvonne: Hoppla, ich bin die einzige Ursache… für die Phänomene meines Lebens. Wie das Gesetz der Annahme mein Leben verändert hat, Independently published, ISBN: 9798620550623.

That is why our message to you is to make yourself aware over and over again: You are the only cause!

State Akin to Sleep

For successful conscious autosuggestion it is essential to "switch off" our will. We achieve this through the state that Neville called "state akin to sleep". It is an important tool, without mastering the state akin to sleep we cannot correctly apply the Law of Assumption. We know this sleep-like state, which is natural for us humans, from the moments just before falling asleep or just after waking up, when we are between waking and sleeping. We experience something similar when we lose ourselves in a daydream.

From our everyday life, we are used to regulating things with our will. Now, however, we have the situation that we only strengthen the situation we are currently in with our willpower. However, since we want to consciously change our situation, we must go into the state akin to sleep before we can start with conscious autosuggestion or prayer, as Neville Goddard and Joseph Murphy called it. We are in this state when we feel tired and exhausted, but also – as already mentioned – in the evening before going to sleep and in the morning after waking up. Therefore, it is also ideal to use these times for conscious autosuggestion.

But we can also create this state consciously, for this purpose we withdraw to a quiet place and go into silence. We sit or lie down comfortably and make sure that we remain undisturbed for the next while. Then we concentrate only on our breath. If thoughts still arise, we let them pass by like clouds in the sky.

We continue to focus on our breath until we feel the body and mind becoming more and more still. Many beginners find it difficult to get into the state akin to sleep and/or relaxation at the beginning. This is normal and no reason to worry. If this is the case for you, then stay consistent, because practice makes perfect.

Visualisation (Scene Technique)

The scene technique is probably the technique most often mentioned technique by Neville Goddard. In the state akin to sleep, we imagine a scene that presupposes the fulfilment of our wish. A scene that we would, even would have to, experience after the fulfilment of our wish. To use Neville's words, *"The end is where we begin."* So first we must be clear about what exactly we want, what we really desire. We need to explore the state we want to achieve (such as being happy, being free, etc.). So, we must ask ourselves: *What do I really want?*

Then we create a scene that would naturally follow the fulfilment of our wish. Neville favoured the so-called congratulatory scene. Here, in our imagination, a person we know congratulates us on the fulfilment of our wish. This scene should never last longer than a few seconds and can include a hug, a handshake, or the clinking of champagne glasses during a toast – in short: something that "seals" our success.

Another possibility would be the telephone scene, which Neville also liked to use very much – especially when he imagined on behalf of others. He would simply imagine the person calling him and telling him about their success (wish fulfilled). Of course, this also works in the other direction: We imagine telling a friend or relative about our fulfilled wish on the phone.

Important: We always see the scene from our own eyes – we do not look at it as a third party from the outside. We can ask ourselves the following questions to work out our scene:

- What would I experience?
- What would have my special attention?

- What do I like about what I see, hear, smell, taste, feel or think?

- What would be different in contrast to how I feel right now?

(... if my wish had already been fulfilled.)

Once we have created a (short!) scene, we enter the state akin to sleep and let it play repeatedly. If we drift off, we gently bring ourselves back to our scene.

This was an excerpt from the book "Simply Manifesting" by Katrine Hütterer and Yvonne Kalb, which I would like to warmly recommend to you. You will also find detailed instructions on other methods by Neville Goddard such as the Lullaby Method, the Fishing Method, the Remember When Method or the Revision Method.

The Letter from Your Future

Now you have basically learned how to create your dream life. The most important ingredient is consistency.

So, what else can you do to support this process over a long period of time?

One method that has proven successful is to write yourself a letter from the future.

Get a nice notebook, a pad or the beautiful workbook from Katy and Yvonne.[22]

Then find a quiet, beautiful place, relax, and take your time. Go in your imagination about five years

---

[22] Hütterer Katrine/Kalb, Yvonne: Manifest Your Dream Life. Write Your Own Future, Independently published, ISBN: 979-8479092619.

ahead and assume that you have already arrived in your dream life. You have the dream partner, the dream house, the dream car, the dream job, and everything you have ever wished for. Close your eyes and let yourself fall completely into the state.

Now, as your future self, you write a letter to your present self. In this letter you report to yourself how well you are doing and which of your dreams have come true.

It is important that you write by hand (pencil, fountain pen, biros) and not on your mobile phone or computer.

Put the date you are writing in the top corner so that you can retrace your development later.

It could look something like this:

6th of August 2021

Dear Norman,

Today is the sixth of August 2026. I am sitting on the terrace of my villa on Lake Starnberg, watching the sailing boats, and I would like to tell you what happened to me. After reading the book "Imagine and get rich", I thought it wouldn't hurt to give it a try.

I then consistently applied the methods mentioned and achieved small successes relatively quickly. When that worked, I holed myself up in the spa for a day and painted my future in the brightest colours and wrote everything down. And then I began to constantly imagine what it would be like if I had achieved everything.

After some time, I got in touch with a woman from the neighbourhood in a chat group who also works with the LOA. We exchanged ideas, met and it was love at first sight. Today we have been happily married for two years.

We moved in together relatively quickly. Then we "accidentally" got to know a business model with which we could earn a small additional income on the side. We then let it grow in our imagination and it initially developed very well and later rapidly, so that my partner was soon able to give up her job.

Little by little, everything we had imagined together came to pass.

Today we live in a villa on Lake Starnberg, have enough time for sports and fitness, work with friends and go on holidays to the most beautiful places in the world. There are three dream cars in the garage, and we can say we have everything we wished for, are happy and healthy.

Yes, dear Norman. This is what awaits you if you remain consistent. So, dig in and imagine!

I love you!
Norman

Of course, this is only an abbreviated example. When you write the letter to yourself, describe the house, the partner, the boat, the mood, the environment, simply everything you want in as much detail as possible.

So, you do not only write "dream car", but maybe you describe a Porsche 911 Targa in green with brown leather seats, or whatever you'd like.

If you don't want a car, you can of course wish for a horse and describe it in detail (breed, colour, size, etc.). Or whatever else you want – hopefully you understand what I mean.

The "trick" in writing the letter is that you go into the state of fulfilled desire (as long as you are writing) for a longer period of time and also put your wishes on paper.

It is recommended that you repeat this exercise (at least) once a month. That's why you have a notebook, so you can keep track of changes.

Maybe new wishes will come, maybe some will change. Basically, it is a recalibration, as if you were checking whether the direction of the compass is still correct.

After half a year, you can also increase the intervals between letter-writing.

Your Gratitude Journal

*„In every exalted joy, there mingles
a sense of gratitude."
Marie von Ebner-Eschenbach*

Another helpful method is writing a gratitude journal. Here you will find the chapter "The Magic of Gratitude" from Katy's book "Manifestiere dich glücklich und frei" (currently only available in German, but keep your eyes open for an upcoming translation), which I find quite wonderful and may include here with her permission:

Many thousands of years ago, gratitude was already mentioned in the oldest records of mankind and has remained an important part of all religions and cultures worldwide. I was also able to experience how the daily practice of gratitude changed my life for the better. Until today, every evening I write down ten things in my gratitude journal for which I am grateful.

Practising gratitude has positive effects on our health, our quality of life, and our brain. This has been scientifically proven. Researchers like Robert Emmons and Michael McCullogh have studied gratitude and conducted many studies on the subject. Among other things, they found that gratitude leads to "positive affective states" and increases "prosocial behaviour". The participants in the study were more optimistic, their physical complaints were reduced, and the researchers came to the conclusion that gratitude "also ensures greater well-being in chronically ill people."[23]

Gratitude not only improves our quality of life with a sustainable and measurable effect, but it can also be

---

[23] Emmons, Robert A./ McCullough, Michael E.: Counting Blessings versus Burdens: An Experimental Investigation of Gratitude and Subjective Well-Being in Daily Life.

applied at any time and by anyone. Gratitude is free of charge! Strictly speaking, it is even a gift to yourself and subsequently to the world. This is because the gratitude you practise triggers a wave, soon spreads to every area of your life, and thus quickly reaches your environment, which reflects this gratitude back to you. This often happens so quickly that it seems like magic.

I personally got to know the practice of gratitude many years ago during my training as a mental & consciousness trainer and find it an important basis for living with one's own creative power. Why? Well, according to science, we think about sixty thousand thoughts a day and about eleven million sensory impressions are processed by our brain every second, but we only consciously perceive about forty of them.[24]

---

[24] https://austria-forum.org/ and https://www.abzaustria.at/, as of 27th of April 2020 or https://medium.com/desk-of-van-schneider/if-you-want-it-you-might-get-it-the-reticular-activating-system-explained-761b6ac14e53, as of 20th of September 2021.

If we were all to perceive consciously, our heads would simply burst. Our brain extracts from the available impressions what we see and (want to) believe. This is done with the help of the reticular activating system (RAS), which acts as a kind of filter and divides our sensory impressions into either new, emotional, or vital information. RAS constantly searches for information that is already consistent with our beliefs and convictions. We all know this: For example, we decide to buy a car of a certain brand and colour. Suddenly we see this car driving or parked everywhere around us. Or when we wish for a relationship, we suddenly see only couples in love everywhere. RAS ensures that we focus our attention on situations in which we receive confirmation of what we are constantly preoccupied with in our thoughts. Of course, this is true in both, a positive and a negative sense. So, when we feel small and insignificant ("I am not worthy ..."), RAS helps us to focus on that, while the people for whom happiness seems to just fly by are also led there by their own assumptions and the reticular activation system.

So, what does this have to do with gratitude practice? We train our RAS in a playful and easy way to present us positive situations for which we can be grateful. If you have been living with blocking beliefs and negative assumptions about yourself for decades, it doesn't help to tell yourself positive affirmations every day. No one can believe themselves if they have thought of themselves as a worthless loser their whole life and suddenly tell themselves every day, "I am a successful millionaire." That definitely doesn't work. But we can choose to find ten reasons each day why we should be grateful. We can start with small things. Do you have a roof over your head? Sufficient food? Clothes? Friends? A family? Are you healthy? Is the sun shining? Has someone invited you for a coffee? Do you hear the birds singing? Has someone given you a smile? Write it down on your list!

We start our daily gratitude practice by writing in our gratitude journal: "I am grateful that ...". Then we note ten things, people, or situations for which we are grateful. I recommend that you also write down things or situations that are currently a burden in everyday life and express them positively. So, for example, if our relationship is difficult right now, we consistently write "I am grateful that my relationship is so happy and harmonious". We do this until something changes. If we feel grateful on the inside, then sooner or later – not least thanks to RAS – the outside will follow.

Neville Goddard also spoke about gratitude in his „Core Lectures": *"My third way of praying is simply to feel thankful. If I want something, either for myself or another, I immobilize the physical body, then I produce the state akin to sleep and, in that state, just feel happy, feel thankful, which thankfulness implies realization of what I want. I assume the feeling of the wish fulfilled and with my mind dominated by this single sensation I go to sleep. I need do nothing to make it so, because it is so. My feeling of the wish fulfilled implies it is done.*

All these techniques you can use and change them to fit your temperament. But I must emphasize the necessity of inducing the drowsy state where you can become attentive without effort. A single sensation dominates the mind, if you pray successfully. What would I feel like, now, were I what I want to be? When I know what the feeling would be like I then close my eyes and lose myself in that single sensation and my dimensionally greater Self then builds a bridge of incident to lead me from this present moment to the fulfillment of my mood. That is all you need do. But people have a habit of slighting the importance of simple things."[25]

Start your gratitude practice today and you will have taken the first step towards a wonderful new life of positive experiences.

---

[25] https://freeneville.com/wp-content/uploads/2012/08/Neville-Goddard-PDF-Core-Teachings-4.pdf, as of 19. September 2021.

This was a passage from Katy's book "Manifestiere dich glücklich und frei". She and her colleague Yvonne have also created a beautiful Gratitude Journal.[26]

---

[26] Hütterer, Katrine/Kalb, Yvonne: Life Is Beautiful. Gratitude Journal, Independently published, ISBN: 979-8480989168.

The Best Investment of All

"By far the best investment you can make is in yourself."
Warren Buffet

In a book with the title "Imagine and Grow Rich", a brief look at the optimal investment strategy is of course indispensable.

Some persons will say that tangible assets are the rage: real estate, precious metals, cars, etc. Others focus on securities: shares, government bonds, corporate bonds. Other people are more speculative and buy cryptocurrencies or options.

The masses, however, probably prefer to invest in consumption: holidays, eating out, the latest mobile phone, a subscription here and a subscription there.

While one thousand euros for a new high-tech mobile phone is spent without complaint, one hundred euros invested in health or personal development often seems too expensive.

But think about it: This is the only investment that no one can take away from you. Everything else can become obsolete, broken, go bankrupt or lose its value for other reasons.

If we realise that we are the only cause of what happens to us, then it is only logical that a good investment in ourselves must influence our condition, our external reality and thus also our future.

So, think carefully about whether you are using your resources wisely when you consume material things or whether you could perhaps also invest in your personal development.

Coaching – Sense or Nonsense?

What do Rafael Nadal, Joanne K. Rowling, Lewis Hamilton, Julia Roberts, Cristiano Ronaldo, George Clooney, Rihanna, and Manuel Neuer have in common?

They are world class at what they do.

And what else? They have a coach – or even several.

Almost no one who is top class in any field can reach this and stay there without a coach. Why? Because you can't see yourself from the outside. Because you don't see how you hit in tennis, because you don't recognise where there is still room for improvement or because you are simply "professionally blinkered".

So, if you have certain goals, you should consider, whether you should look out for someone to accompany you in the process.

If you are "stuck" at any point and do not succeed in overcoming some thresholds (for example: you never manage to save more than ten thousand euros or you never manage more than five thousand euros turnover per month in your business), then it is quite possible that limiting beliefs are working in your subconscious, or experiences from childhood that you have long forgotten, which are sabotaging your success.

In such a case, a one-time session with a (good!) coach may already break the knot.

Either way, it makes sense to surround yourself with like-minded people. You can share your successes – and staying engaged with the topic will also help you stay consistent.

By the way, with the help of the Law of Assumption you can also imagine that you have already found the ideal coach for you. And you will then certainly come across one "by chance"' or be told about one by someone or read an article ...

I can guarantee you from my own experience that you will get further with the occasional support of an experienced coach than without.

Afterword

We hope you enjoyed our book and were able to gain new insights, tips, or ideas.

We would be very happy to receive a positive review of this book, as it will rank higher then and allow even more people to learn about this wonderful concept. Thank you very much for this.

And we would also like to thank *you* for working on yourself and your further development and thus making the world a better place.

And don't forget: **Everything is possible for those who believe.**

We wish you the very best for your life!

Katy & Norman

Dear reader!

If you enjoyed this book and it inspired you to finally create the life of your dreams, we would be very happy to
receive a positive review.

Thank you very much!

Recommended Literature

Berlay, Louise: The Magic of the Mind: How To Do What You Want With Your Life, Audio Enlightenment, ISBN: 978-1941489321.

Byrne, Rhonda: The Secret, Simon & Schuster UK, ISBN: 978-1847370297.

Coué, Émile: Self-Mastery Through Conscious Autosuggestion, G&D Media, ISBN: 978-1722502638.

Goddard, Neville: The Complete Reader, Audio Enlightenment; Illustrated Edition, ISBN: 978-0991091409.

Haanel, Charles F.: The Master Key System, SoHo Books, ISBN: 978-1612930831.

Hill, Napoleon: Think and Grow Rich, Wilder Publications, ISBN: 978-1604591873.

Hütterer, Katrine/Kalb, Yvonne: Create the Life You Want. Manifestation Journal, Independently published, ISBN: 979-8479560033.

Hütterer, Katrine/Kalb, Yvonne: Life Is Beautiful. Gratitude Journal, Independently published, ISBN: 979-8480989168.

Hütterer Katrine/Kalb, Yvonne: Manifest Your Dream Life. Write Your Own Future, Independently published, ISBN: 979-8479092619.

Hütterer, Katrine/Kalb, Yvonne: Simply Manifesting: The Law of Assumption Easily Explained, Independently published, ISBN: 979-8476407959.

Murphy, Joseph: The Power of Your Subconscious Mind: Unlock the Secrets Within, TarcherPerigee, ISBN: 978-1585427680.

Schwarzenegger, Arnold: Total Recall: My Unbelievably True Life Story, Simon & Schuster, ISBN: 978-1451662443.

Wattles, Wallace D.: The Science of Getting Rich, CreateSpace Independent Publishing Platform, ISBN: 978-1490471761.

About Norman P. Fischer

Behind the pseudonym Norman P. Fischer hides a successful German businessman.

Norman P. Fischer studied business administration and has experienced all the ups and downs of business life. For 20 years he has been dealing with the question "How success is created and what sabotages it".

He describes "Imagine and Grow Rich" as a "What-you-must-consider-book". It is his second publication after his first book "Manifestieren mit Tabellen".

About Katrine Hütterer

Katrine Hütterer, M.A., studied journalism and communication science and worked as a journalist for many years. In her mid-thirties, she experienced a burnout because, as a perfectionist, she constantly put herself under pressure and overtaxed herself.

Many coachings and trainings in the field of life support and (mental) coaching as well as a professional reorientation were the result.

Today she is an author, editor, and mentor. Together with her colleague Yvonne Kalb, she forms Team Huetterer. They both love and live the gratitude practice and the art of manifesting with the Law of Assumption (LOA) according to Neville Goddard.

The authors do not assume any liability for the topicality, correctness, completeness, or quality of the information provided. Liability claims against the authors relating to material or non-material damage caused by the use or non-use of the information provided or using incorrect or incomplete information are fundamentally excluded unless there is evidence of wilful intent or gross negligence on the part of the authors.

First publication in English

September 2021

www.katrinehuetterer.com

www.team-huetterer.com

Printed in Great Britain
by Amazon